Color God's Creation

Artwork by Caroline Simas

HARVEST HOUSE PUBLISHERS
EUGENE, OREGON

Cover by Katie Brady Design

COLOR GOD'S CREATION

Copyright © 2016 Caroline Simas
Published by Harvest House Publishers
Eugene, Oregon 97402
www.harvesthousepublishers.com

ISBN 978-0-7369-6884-3 (pbk.)

Printed in the United States of America

16 17 18 19 20 21 22 23 24 / VP-CD / 10 9 8 7 6 5 4 3

A Good Place to Begin

This coloring book is for artists of all ages and talents, and that means you! Let your creative spirit free, choose any color you like, and make each beautiful image your own. There are no rules except to have fun.

Enjoy the process. Feel free to use colored pencils, pens, watercolors, markers, and crayons—or any combination thereof—to add color and texture to each design. Notice that all the pictures are printed on just one side of the paper. To keep colors from bleeding through to the next page, simply slip an extra piece of paper underneath the page you're working on. When finished, you might like to remove the page from the book, trim it to size, and frame your artwork for all to see.

Most importantly, have fun with the process. Enjoy experimenting with contrasting colors or different shades of the same color. Try lighter hues for a softer look or layer and blend your colors for even more options. Allow some white space or saturate the entire piece with rich, vibrant color, depending on your mood. Let your worries go, relax in the moment, and allow your creative spirit to lead the way!

Through him all things were made; without him nothing was made that has been made.

John 1:3

The Lord is my strength and my shield...my heart leaps for joy, and with my song I praise him.

Psalm 28:7

In his hand is the life of every creature and the breath of all mankind.
Job 12:10

This is the day that the
Lord has made;
let us rejoice and be glad in it.
Psalm 118:24

The earth is the LORD's and all that is in it, the world, and those who live in it; for he has founded it on the seas, and established it on the rivers.
Psalm 24:1-2

The heavens are Yours, the earth also is Yours; The world and all it contains, You have founded them. Psalm 89:11

He determines the number of the stars; he gives to all of them their names.

Psalm 147:4

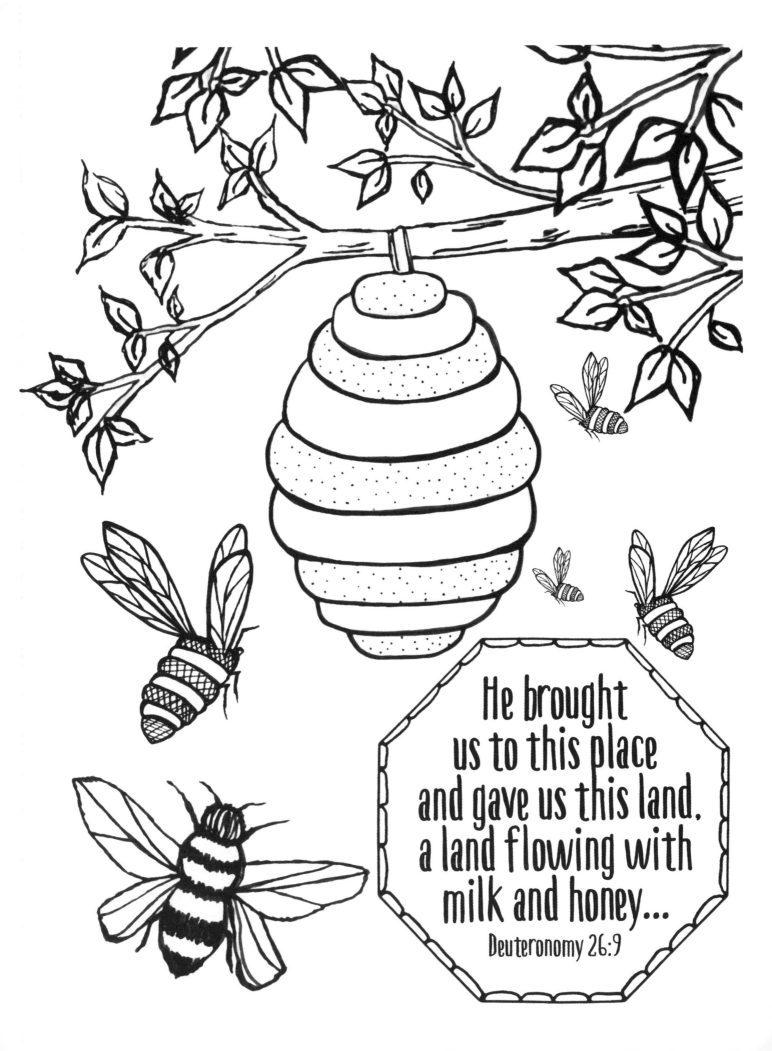

He brought us to this place and gave us this land, a land flowing with milk and honey...

Deuteronomy 26:9

Gracious words are a honeycomb, sweet to the soul and healing to the bones.

Proverb 16:24

He
has made
EVERYTHING
BEAUTIFUL
in its time.

Ecclesiastes 3:11

2 Samuel 23:4

He is like the light of morning at sunrise on a cloudless morning, like the brightness after rain that brings grass from the earth.

Bless the LORD, O my soul.
O LORD my God, you are very great. You are clothed with
honor and majesty, wrapped in light as with a garment. You stretch out the
heavens like a tent, you set the beams of your chambers on the waters, you make
the clouds your chariot, you ride on the wings of the wind, you make the winds
your messengers, fire and flame your ministers. You set the earth on its
foundations, so that it shall never be shaken. You cover it with the deep as
with a garment; the waters stood above the mountains.

Psalm 104:1-6

Wait for the Lord;
be strong and
take heart...

Psalm 27:14

O Lord, it is You who made
the heaven and the earth and the sea,
and all that is in them...
Acts 4:24

In his hand are the depths
of the earth...
Psalm 95:4

He draws up
the drops of water,
which distill as rain to the streams;
the clouds pour down their moisture and
abundant showers fall on mankind...

Job 36:27-28

As the RAIN and the SNOW come down from heaven, and do not return to it without watering the earth and making it bud and flourish...

Isaiah 55:10

Be completely humble and gentle; be patient, bearing with one another in love.

Ephesians 4:2

How much better to get *wisdom* than gold, to get insight rather than silver! Proverbs 16:16

Let EVERYTHING that has breath praise the Lord.

Psalm 150:6

For everything God created is good, and nothing is to be rejected if it is received with thanksgiving...

1 Timothy 4:4

Every good and perfect gift is from above.

James 1:17

I am the vine;
you are the branches.
If you remain in me and I
in you, you will bear
much fruit;

apart from me
you can do nothing.
John 15:5

"For I know the plans I have for you," declares the Lord, "plans to prosper you and not to harm you, plans to give you hope and a future."

Jeremiah 29:11

Yours, O LORD, are the greatness, the power, the glory, the victory, and the majesty: for all that is in the heavens and on the earth is yours...

1 Chronicles 29:11

The grass withers,
the flower fades, but
the word of our God
will stand forever.

Isaiah 40:8